KETO

VEGAN

COOKBOOK

Nutritious Plant-Based, Dairy-Free, Low-Carb Recipes for a Ketogenic Diet

Jennifer Tate

Contents

Introduction

I would like you to pause for a moment and think about the foods that you grew up eating.

Did you get fast food on the way home from school? Did your parents grab a pack of hotdogs from the freezer when running low on time?

Have you ever taken a step back and thought about how scary it is that our modern diets are so unhealthy and lacking in nutrition? We often rely on quick and easy foods that contain ingredients we don't even know how to pronounce and astonishingly high amounts of sugar and salt that are massive causes of the most common life-threatening diseases like hypertension, type 2 diabetes, and cancer.

Veganism has steadily gained more traction over the years, and there's a good reason for that. Not only is it easier than ever to find delicious, fully vegan recipes and ingredients, but the numerous health benefits of Veganism are the main reason why more and more people are flocking to this lifestyle.

Keto Veganism is a step up from simple Veganism, and I'm here to tell you all the 'whys' and 'hows' of this highly nutritious, modified lifestyle.

So how did I personally start on this journey?

Honestly, the beginning was a bit of a chore at first, mainly because I had to Google everything, I even thought of putting it in my mouth beforehand to make sure that it fell into both categories of being vegan and Keto at the same time. I, of course, didn't have a handy little book to help me clearly understand what I could and couldn't eat, so I would waste an excessive amount of time looking up all my ingredients.

On top of those immediate effects, both Veganism and Keto are proven to lower cholesterol and high blood pressure and reduce your risk of heart disease, diabetes, and cancer.

With all this being said, here are the things I hope you take away from this book:

- What Keto Veganism is and how it works to improve your overall health.
- That vegan food isn't boring like many seem to think—you won't be eating lettuce three times a day, every day; I promise.
- A good idea of what foods are both Keto and vegan-friendly, and not having to stress about not dieting correctly.
- How to start and keep the ball rolling on your new journey.

So, let's take a deeper look into this fascinating lifestyle!

Keto Vegan Basics

So, what is Keto Veganism?

Well, let's start by explaining what each diet is separately.

Veganism is a diet in which a vegan will only eat plant-based foods.

It has been around for decades and has become increasingly more common and even encouraged in recent years due to its health benefits and impact on society. Vegans do not eat any animal products whatsoever—this includes things like dairy products and honey. It's also an entire lifestyle, rather than simply being a healthy diet, in which a practicing Vegan will refuse to use any products tested on animals or contain any animal by-products, such as wool, leather, or fur. There are a ton of other social implications of the vegan lifestyle, but for the sake of this book, we will mostly stick to the diet side.

The Ketogenic diet (or just the Keto) is a low-carb, high-fat diet.

When you're on the Keto diet, your goal is for your daily meals only to contain a small amount of carbohydrates while increasing fat and protein content. This leads to a process called Ketosis, where your body begins to burn fat instead of glucose, leading to weight loss. That means no bread and other flour-based products, which are high in carbohydrates, and a limited amount of grains, legumes, and root vegetables, which usually play a big part in a regular vegan diet.

So, since Veganism relies heavily on grains and other high-carb plant products, can the two diets be combined effectively?

Of course! I wouldn't be writing this book if it wasn't!

The biggest part of successfully doing Keto Veganism is that it is crucial that you plan ahead and you are aware of what is and isn't allowed. This book is designed to educate you and help you take the first few steps without stressing whether you're doing it correctly.

How Does It Work?

I will get just a little bit science-y here but stay with me. I want you to understand exactly what processes your body goes through when implementing this diet.

When you eat carbs, your body converts those carbs into glucose, which is used to fuel your body and give you energy. The leftover glucose that isn't converted to energy gets stored in your liver as glycogen, which converts back into glucose throughout the day or whenever necessary. If, for example, you don't eat for a couple of days, your body will run out of glucose and be forced to find another energy source. Your body will then break down fat stores and use those broken-down molecules, along with proteins and amino acids, as the necessary fuel to keep you going. Since you're burning fat for energy instead of glucose, you will likely lose weight.

This process is called Ketosis and is the defining point of the Keto diet.

For the majority of people, limiting your *carbohydrate intake to under 50 g per day* is enough to start the process of Ketosis and keep it going, but some people prefer to limit it to as low as 20 g per day. The basic rule is that only 5-10% of your daily caloric intake should be carbs, but we all know that sometimes our total calories equal more or less than the previous day, so it's far easier and more beneficial to decide on an amount in grams rather than focusing on percentage.

On the other hand, you also have the science behind Veganism. It's a known fact that plant-based foods are high in vitamins and nutrients, so by cutting out meat and dairy—both of which are usually the highest calorie foods in a meal—you will be substituting those missed calories with much more plant-based foods, leading to more nutrients that are great for your body.

An upside of Keto Veganism is that you have a limited amount of foods you can eat while on the diet. Now, that may sound like a bad thing at first, but a limited amount of ingredients doesn't mean a limited amount of recipes. As a quick example, spinach is a great food packed with multiple types of vitamins, iron, and calcium. Using spinach, you can make a whole array of Keto Vegan recipes from green smoothies to quiches to salads and even cream spinach (with a substitute for dairy products, of course). In fact, for many of us in this busy world, having a limited list of ingredients to choose from decides what to eat so much easier and more streamlined than worrying about how many carbs or fats are in every meal.

So, don't get too hung up about being restricted. It can be more of a blessing than a curse.

How to Get Started

There are three main ways you can go about starting your journey with Keto Veganism:

- Go vegan first
- Start the Keto diet first
- Or take the plunge and go straight into both at the same time.

Choosing how to start largely depends on your current lifestyle.

- If you're already a vegetarian or even a pescatarian, switching to veganism is recommended. Once you've tried it out for a few days or weeks (or even months; everyone moves at their own pace) and you've become comfortable with the vegan lifestyle, you can slowly start eliminating or limiting the high-carb foods in your diet. This is likely the easiest and smoothest way to transition to Keto as well.

- On the other hand, if you are a total carnivore and love your meat, starting with Keto would be a better option. Meat is not high in carbs, so the Keto diet does not shun it. So, if you can cut out things like bread, rice, potatoes, and other high-carb fillers, starting Keto (and achieving Ketosis) is possible. Once you've mastered the Keto diet, tweaking it to Keto Veganism will be much easier.

There is also the option of jumping headfirst into Keto Veganism, although I would not recommend this. If you feel like you can do it this way, then, by all means, go for it! For most people, however, changing your diet, especially if you've been eating a certain way for many years, is a long process. Some people can immediately cut out meat and carbs cold turkey and be completely happy and healthy in their new diet, but others will need to start reducing those foods gradually.

If you're scared to go vegan, cut out red meat slowly. When you feel like you're ready for the next step, cut out white meat and keep going until you reach your goal of veganism.

The same goes for Keto. Many of us tend to eat bread, rice, or other high-carb foods with our meals, so I recommend reducing the amount of your chosen starch with each meal and replacing it with other foods until you've managed to eliminate it or greatly reduce your intake of these foods.

You understand the end goal, but how you reach that goal is entirely up to you and what you feel will be best for yourself. So, draw up a personalized plan, take time, and be nice to yourself.

You'll get there.

What to Eat on the Keto Vegan Diet?

As mentioned before, being on a vegan diet means consuming only plant-based products. This includes things such as fruits, vegetables, seeds, nuts, beans, and grains. If nothing in the meal has come from or is produced by an animal, you're okay on the vegan end.

Just as a side note: when I say 'produced by' an animal, I mean that vegans don't consume any animal products, regardless of whether the animal was harmed or not. For example: honey or dairy products. While the production of these products does not directly involve any animal cruelty, the fact that bees and cows must work for our benefit is seen as a type of animal slavery and is frowned upon in the vegan community.

Once you've narrowed your diet down to vegan, you must decide on your daily carbohydrate intake (remember, it's usually between 20 and 50 grams) and then focus on eating plant-based foods low in carbs.

Another side note: Protein is an important part of the Keto diet, so it is important to note that while beans and legumes might be higher in carbs than things like fruits and leafy vegetables, they're also higher in protein and should not be excluded from the diet to drop your daily carbohydrate intake even lower. A balance is needed.

Keto also places a lot of importance on fat. In fact, it is recommended that your meals consist of 70-80% fat. In this specific diet, you will get the highest percentage of fats from the available oils, nuts, seeds, and certain fruits, such as avocados.

I've added a table below to give you an idea of the most easily accessible low-carb ingredients you should use while on the Keto Vegan diet. I hope this makes it much easier for you to plan your meals while knowing exactly what you're taking in.

Food	Net Carbohydrates (Grams per 1 Cup)	Food	Net Carbohydrates (Grams per 1 Cup)
Almond	12 g	Kale	4 g
Almond Butter	28 g	Kiwi	16 g
Almond Milk (Unsweetened)	2 g	Lemon	8 g

Apples	16 g	Lentils	24 g
Arugula	5 g	Lettuce	4 g
Asparagus	5 g	Macadamia Nuts	7 g
Avocados	2 g	Olives	4 g
Bell Peppers	8 g	Olive Oil	0 g
Black Beans	26 g	Onions	10 g
Black Soybeans	20 g	Oranges	12 g
Blackberries	6 g	Peaches	10 g
Blueberries	16 g	Peanut Butter (Natural)	32 g
Brazilian Nuts	5 g	Peanuts	18 g
Broccoli	5 g	Pears	16 g
Brussel Sprouts	7 g	Peas	20 g
Cabbage	4 g	Pecan Nuts	5 g
Canola Oil	0 g	Pineapples	16 g
Cantaloupe	9 g	Pinto Beans	25 g
Carrots	9 g	Plums	13 g
Cauliflower	4 g	Radish	4 g
Celery	4 g	Raspberries	7 g
Cherries	13 g	Soy Milk	15 g
Chia Seeds	10 g	Spinach	5 g

Chickpeas	26 g	Strawberries	7 g
Clementines	13 g	Sucralose	0 g
Coconut	8 g	Sunflower Seed Butter	16 g
Coconut Milk	13 g	Swiss Chard	5 g
Coconut Oil	0 g	Tahini	32 g
Coffee	0 g	Tea	0 g
Cucumber	5 g (3 g Peeled)	Tofu Extra Firm	6 g
Edamame Beans	11 g	Tomatoes	3 g
Eggplant	4 g	Vegetable Oil	0 g
Flax Seeds	3 g	Walnut	9 g
Green Beans	5 g	Watermelon	10 g
Hazelnuts	9 g	Wine (Dry Red)	3 g
Hemp Seeds	8 g	White Mushrooms	2 g
Honeydew Melon	11 g	Zucchini	4 g

While knowing what foods are okay to eat on this diet, it's also important to know what's not okay.

Non-vegan foods that you should avoid:

- Meat of any kind. That includes red meat, white meat, fish, and shellfish.
- Dairy products such as milk, cheese, butter, and cream.
- Eggs or products that contain eggs, like mayonnaise.

- Certain candies which contain gelatin.
- Honey.

Non-Keto foods that you should avoid or limit:

- Grains should be generally avoided or highly limited. These include rice, bread, pasta, tortillas, and even more healthy options like quinoa.
- Root vegetables like potatoes, sweet potatoes, yams, and parsnips.
- Some fruits, such as bananas, raisins, dates, and mangoes.
- Corn and products that contain corn.
- Beer (it is interesting to note that most other non-sugary alcoholic drinks are pretty low in carbs, by contrast).
- Fruit and vegetable juice. That might sound weird, and juices don't contain a lot of carbs, but they do contain liquid carbs. Liquid carbs absorb into your body very quickly and often lead to a spike in your blood sugar levels, which is something you should always try to avoid while doing Keto.

So, with all this acquired knowledge, you are now well-equipped to start your new life journey!

Breakfast Recipes

If you're anything like me, you wake up ravenous. I must have smart options available to prevent myself from sabotaging my keto dreams first thing in the day. Luckily, there are sweet and savory options available.

Vanilla Cinnamon Muffins

Stir-Fried Tofu

Nut Granola

Comfort Breakfast

Avocado Shake

American-Style Pancakes

Vanilla Cinnamon Muffins

These are perfect for when you *need* bread but do not need carbohydrates. Almond milk can be used as a substitute for soy milk if desired.

Yield: 10 muffins

INGREDIENTS

1 cup almond flour

1 tsp. baking soda

½ tsp. cinnamon

⅓ cup coconut flour

cooking spray (optional)

1 Tbsp. flaxseed flour

¾ cup smooth peanut butter

1 cup (240 ml) soy milk

3 Tbsp. stevia

½ tsp. vanilla bourbon

INSTRUCTIONS

1. Preheat oven to 350°F (180°C).

2. Combine wet ingredients (peanut butter, soy milk, and vanilla bourbon) in a bowl and mix thoroughly with a hand or stand mixer.

3. Combine dry ingredients (almond flour, coconut flour, flaxseed flour, stevia, baking soda, and cinnamon) in a separate bowl and mix thoroughly with a whisk.

4. Pour the mixed bowl of wet ingredients into the bowl of dry ingredients and thoroughly combine.

5. Spray the muffin tin cups with cooking spray or line them with cupcake liners.

6. Use a clean measuring cup to fill the cups to a uniform level.

7. Bake the muffins for about 30 minutes. Check that they are fully cooked by inserting a clean toothpick into the center of a muffin. If it comes out coated with batter, put the tin back in the oven for another few minutes and try again. If the muffins resemble charcoal briquettes, try for 20 minutes the next time.

NUTRITIONAL INFORMATION (PER SERVING)

Calories: 197, Total Carbohydrates: 11.9 g, Dietary Fiber: 2.9 g, Total Sugars: 3.2 g

Stir-Fried Tofu

These can be paired with sugar-free maple syrup or sugar-free chocolate sauce without a large increase in net carbs. As a good rule of thumb, any moisture you can get out of the tofu before you cook is going to make your dish exponentially better.

Yield: 3 servings

INGREDIENTS

1 Tbsp. cinnamon

cooking spray

18 oz. (510 g) block extra firm tofu

4 Tbsp. stevia

INSTRUCTIONS

1. Drain the tofu using a tofu press according to its instructions. If a tofu press is unavailable, wrap the tofu block in a highly absorbent towel (or several layers of paper towels) and allow it to drain on a large plate with a deep lip for 30 minutes, sitting under a weight such as a large frying pan or heavy cans.

2. Combine cinnamon and stevia in a mixing bowl with a whisk.

3. After the tofu has drained (the less moisture, the better), cut it into consistently sized sticks.

4. Sprinkle tofu sticks with a quarter of the cinnamon mixture.

5. Coat a frying pan with cooking spray and turn a burner on low heat.

6. Place the tofu sticks in the pan, taking care to leave space between them.

7. For about 30 minutes, flip tofu sticks to a new side every three to four minutes until they spring back from a touch (they should be very firm). Sprinkle the remainder of the cinnamon mixture after each flip until used completely.

NUTRITIONAL INFORMATION (PER SERVING)

Calories: 125, Total Carbohydrates: 4.7 g, Dietary Fiber: 2.7 g, Total Sugars: 1.1 g

Nut Granola

This pairs very well with almond or soy milk or can be used on plain, dairy-free yogurt as a topper. Flax seeds, hemp seeds, macadamia nuts, peanuts, pine nuts, sesame seeds, and walnuts are all alternative ingredients you can add or substitute for variety.

Yield: 12 servings

INGREDIENTS

⅓ cup (50 g) almonds

¾ cup (100 g) Brazil nuts

3 Tbsp. (30 g) chia seeds

1 tsp. cinnamon

4 Tbsp. cocoa or cacao nibs

3 Tbsp. cocoa powder

¼ cup (60 g) coconut oil

⅓ cup (50 g) hazelnuts

½ cup (60 g) pecans

½ cup (50 g) pumpkin seeds

pinch of salt

¾ cup (130 g) sunflower seeds

4 Tbsp. toasted coconut chips

¼ cup (60 ml) water

INSTRUCTIONS

1. Preheat oven to 350°F (180°C).

2. Use a food processor or high-speed blender to grind the chia seeds into as fine a powder as possible.

3. Add almonds, Brazil nuts, hazelnuts, pecans, pumpkin seeds, and sunflower seeds to the powder, and pulse the blender or food processor a few times to break up the nuts.

4. Transfer the nuts and powder to a mixing bowl.

5. Add cinnamon, toasted cocoa nibs, coconut chips, and a pinch of salt. Stir to combine all the ingredients completely.

6. In a separate bowl, mix the coconut oil and cocoa powder with a whisk.

7. Pour the liquid mixture over the nuts and add water. Coat the nuts thoroughly.

8. Spread the entire mixture evenly onto a baking sheet.

9. Bake for 15-20 minutes. Once or twice, stir the granola and smooth it back out for the remainder.

10. Remove the baking sheet and let the granola cool completely.

11. Store finished granola in an airtight container.

NUTRITIONAL INFORMATION (PER SERVING)

Calories: 290, Total Carbohydrates: 10.9 g, Dietary Fiber: 6.1 g, Total Sugars: 1.3 g

Comfort Breakfast

Warm comfort food hits the spot some mornings, accomplishing that without overloading you with carbohydrates. For more flavor, you can also stir in sugar-free maple syrup or sugar-free brown sugar.

Yield: 2 servings

INGREDIENTS

2 Tbsp. chia seeds

1 tsp. cinnamon

2 Tbsp. ground flaxseed

¼ cup hemp hearts

⅛ tsp. salt

stevia (optional for taste)

½ tsp. vanilla extract

water (optional for texture)

MICROWAVE INSTRUCTIONS

1. Combine chia seeds, ground flaxseed, hemp hearts, and salt in a microwave-safe bowl and stir.

2. Microwave uncovered on high for 60 seconds and stir. Repeat until the oatmeal is to your desired consistency.

3. Stir in cinnamon and vanilla, then add stevia and water to taste.

STOVETOP INSTRUCTIONS

4. Combine chia seeds, ground flaxseed, hemp hearts, salt, stevia, and water in a small saucepan over medium heat.

5. Stir for one minute and break apart any clumps that develop.

6. Bring oatmeal to a simmer, adjust the heat to keep it at a low simmer, and stir regularly.

7. When oatmeal is thickened, remove from heat and stir in cinnamon and vanilla for another minute until well blended.

8. Add in additional water and stevia for taste if desired.

NUTRITIONAL INFORMATION (PER SERVING)

Calories: 168, Total Carbohydrates: 6.1 g, Dietary Fiber: 5.3 g, Total Sugars: 0.3 g

Avocado Shake

Need something minty and vigorous to start your day? This creamy, dairy-free shake is much healthier than its McDonald's namesake!

Yield: 2 servings

INGREDIENTS

- ½ avocado
- 1 cup (240 ml) coconut milk
- 1 cup ice
- maple syrup or stevia (to taste)
- ¼ cup fresh mint leaves (can be increased or decreased to taste)
- 1 tsp. vanilla extract

INSTRUCTIONS

1. Add all the ingredients to a blender or food processor and blend on high until they are thoroughly pureéd and completely smooth.

NUTRITIONAL INFORMATION (PER SERVING)

Calories: 401, Total Carbohydrates: 16.7 g, Dietary Fiber: 6.8 g, Total Sugars: 4.5 g

American-Style Pancakes

A breakfast staple, pancakes are generally verboten when you're trying to maintain ketosis. Luckily, this recipe allows you to have your cake and lose weight too. Almond flour can be used as a substitute for coconut flour.

Yield: 3 pancakes

INGREDIENTS

½ tsp. baking powder

1 Tbsp. coconut flour

1 Tbsp. ground flax

liquid stevia (to taste)

pinch of salt (only if using unsalted almond butter)

2 Tbsp. unsweetened almond butter

¼ cup (60 ml) unsweetened almond milk

vegetable oil of choice

INSTRUCTIONS

1. On low-medium heat, warm a frying pan and lightly coat it with vegetable oil.

2. Combine the almond butter and milk in a small bowl and set aside.

3. In a separate bowl, combine the baking powder, coconut flour, ground flax, and salt. Blend well.

4. Blend wet and dry ingredients and mix thoroughly.

5. Let the batter sit for three to five minutes to thicken.

6. Scoop the batter into the heated skillet and delicately smooth it into a pancake shape. If you have trouble spreading the batter, wet the back of a spatula with warm water and smear the batter into shape.

7. Cook on low-medium heat for three minutes, and wiggle the spatula under the pancake to gauge how well done it is. It may need to be cooked for four to five minutes. As with traditional pancakes, the surface will populate with small bubbles when it's ready to be flipped.

8. After the underside has reached a golden color, flip the pancake and cook for two to three more minutes.

NUTRITIONAL INFORMATION (PER SERVING)

Calories: 102, Total Carbohydrates: 6.2 g, Dietary Fiber: 2.8 g, Total Sugars: 0.9 g

Main Dishes

When you're ready for a full meal, finding options that cater to your specific vegan and keto needs can be difficult. Luckily, we've found over a dozen possibilities to keep you full and in ketosis.

Stuffed Spaghetti Squash with Cashew Ricotta and Marinara Sauce

Traditional Vegan Meatballs

Cauliflower Falafel Balls

Cauliflower & Broccoli with Tahini Sauce

Baked Cauliflower Florets

Mexican Chili Stew

Stir-Fried Mushrooms with Vegetables

Grilled Eggplant

Bigos with Mushrooms

Vegan Mushroom Shepherd's Pie

Fried Shirataki Noodles with Broccolini

Grilled Marinated Mushrooms

Stuffed Spaghetti Squash with Cashew Ricotta and Marinara Sauce

Keto fare can be hard to get a hold of, and vegan fare can be just as hard to get a hold of, so when you're looking for both in the same dish, it can feel like hunting for leprechauns. It's good to have DIY recipes in your arsenal that can be created from more easily obtained ingredients. This spaghetti squash can be made with store-bought vegan ricotta and low-carb marinara, but these marinara and ricotta recipes are options if you can't find them elsewhere and are versatile enough to be used in different recipes.

Yield: 2 servings

CASHEW RICOTTA INGREDIENTS

¾ tsp. apple cider vinegar

1 garlic clove

¾ tsp. nutritional yeast

⅛ tsp. onion powder

6 Tbsp. raw cashews

¼ tsp. sea salt

2 Tbsp. water

CASHEW RICOTTA INSTRUCTIONS

1. Let the cashews soak in a bowl of water for at least two hours. Letting them soak in boiling water for five minutes is a faster method.

2. After the cashews have soaked, drain them, and put all ingredients in a food processor or high-speed blender. Integrate thoroughly, often stopping to scrape the sides down. Continue until the mix is creamy.

3. Scoop the mixture into an airtight container and place it in the refrigerator for two hours to allow it to thicken. If it is too thick, add a few drops of water at a time, mixing until it's your desired consistency. Stir well before using.

MARINARA INGREDIENTS

1 bay leaf

black pepper (to taste)

7 oz. (200 g) canned crushed tomatoes

1 finely minced garlic clove

¼ Tbsp. olive oil

¼ tsp. oregano

pinch of red pepper flakes

salt (to taste)

MARINARA INSTRUCTIONS

4. In a cold saucepan, combine the garlic, olive oil, and red pepper flakes and put them to medium heat. Stirring regularly, heat for about one minute until the garlic sizzles, but before it browns.

5. Pour in the tomatoes, then add the bay leaf, black pepper, oregano, and salt. Mix in spices and garlic throughout the tomatoes.

6. Reduce heat from medium to low and allow the sauce to simmer for 20 minutes. To keep the sauce from sticking to the bottom of the pan, stir every few minutes and make sure it isn't boiling too high. It should be bubbling but not splashing on your stovetop.

7. After removing the saucepan from the heat, stir and extract the bay leaf before serving.

SPAGHETTI SQUASH INGREDIENTS

½ cup baby greens, such as spinach or arugula

½ cup cashew ricotta cheese

crumbled cashew ricotta cheese (for topping)

1 cup (240 ml) marinara sauce

1 spaghetti squash

SPAGHETTI SQUASH INSTRUCTIONS

8. Preheat oven to 350°F (180°C).

9. Cut spaghetti squash in half lengthwise. Remove squash seeds; an ice cream scoop works better than a spoon.

10. Glaze the insides of the squash with olive oil and sprinkle with pepper and salt.

11. Place the squash on a baking sheet, cut side down, and bake for 40 - 50 minutes or until you can penetrate the skin with a fork.

12. Remove the baking sheet from the oven and let the squash sit for about 10 minutes.

13. Set the oven to broil.

14. After the squash has cooled, scrape the interiors with a fork, not tearing the skins. This will create the spaghetti-like strands that squash is famous for.

15. In a large bowl, combine the baby greens, marinara sauce, strands of spaghetti squash, and ricotta.

16. Ladle the squash mixture into the bottom of the squash halves.

17. Sprinkle some of the crumbled ricotta over the top of each squash mixture.

18. Broil the filled squash until the ricotta on the top reaches a golden brown. It takes about 5 - 7 minutes.

NUTRITIONAL INFORMATION (PER SERVING)

Calories: 357, Total Carbohydrates: 40 g, Dietary Fiber: 4.7 g, Total Sugars: 6.9 g

Traditional Vegan Meatballs

Believe it or not, even though these 'meatballs' have a ground beef texture and are covered in gravy, they are indeed vegan. They're also easily paired with zoodles, mashed turnips, or cauliflower as keto-friendly side dishes.

Yield: 20 meatballs

INGREDIENTS

¼ tsp. allspice

¼ tsp. black pepper (plus more to taste)

½ cup chopped celery

1 Tbsp. cornstarch

1 tsp. Dijon mustard

3 Tbsp. dried minced onions

2 tsp. dried parsley

½ cup dry chickpeas

1 tsp. garlic powder

13.5 oz. (400 ml) low-fat coconut milk

4 minced garlic cloves

¼ tsp. nutmeg

1 tsp. onion powder

1½ cups roughly chopped mushrooms

3 - 4 Tbsp. soy sauce

1 cup (240 ml) unsweetened almond milk

¾ cup unsweetened coconut flakes

1⅞ cup (450 ml) water

2 Tbsp. cold water

5 tsp. vegan Worcestershire sauce

INSTRUCTIONS

1. Preheat oven to 425°F.

2. Over medium heat in a medium-sized saucepan, sauté the onions in three tablespoons of water until the onions are translucent. Add more water if needed to keep the onions from sticking to the pan.

3. Add the garlic and sauté for two to three more minutes.

4. Add the chickpeas and one and a half cups of water. Bring the mixture to a boil and let it simmer for 15 to 20 minutes. Chickpeas should have absorbed liquids and become tender.

5. In a frying pan over medium heat, sauté the mushrooms in three tablespoons of water for five minutes.

6. Grind the unsweetened coconut flakes into flour in a food processor or high-speed blender.

7. Add the allspice, chickpeas, mushrooms, nutmeg, parsley, pepper, soy sauce, and Worcestershire sauce to the food processor/ blender and blend them until they're thoroughly combined, but don't overmix into mush. You want some texture from the chickpeas and mushrooms to remain.

8. Taste and add more pepper and/or soy sauce if desired.

9. Let the mixture sit for 15 minutes to thicken.

10. Place a silicone baking mat or parchment paper on a baking sheet.

11. Roll the mixture into meatballs and place on the baking sheet.

12. Bake for 10 minutes, flip each ball, then bake for 10 to 15 minutes more.

13. While the meatballs bake, add the almond milk, coconut milk, garlic powder, mustard, onion powder, soy sauce, and Worcestershire sauce into a medium-sized saucepan.

14. Bring the saucepan to a simmer over medium heat, and stir occasionally. Remove from heat and add pepper to taste.

15. Whisk the cornstarch and two tablespoons of cold water in a small bowl to create a slushy texture and blend it into the saucepan mixture.

16. Return the saucepan to medium heat and bring it back to a simmer. The gravy should be thick; if it's too thin, add more cornstarch slush.

17. Serve the gravy over the meatballs.

NUTRITIONAL INFORMATION (PER SERVING)

Calories: 99, Total Carbohydrates: 6.5 g, Dietary Fiber: 2.1 g, Total Sugars: 1.8 g

Cauliflower Falafel Balls

This recipe is great if you're craving something with a little Middle Eastern flair. Serve them with lettuce, sprouts, and tomatoes without significantly increasing your carb intake.

Yield: 16 falafels

NUTRITIONAL INFORMATION (PER SERVING)

Calories: 18, Total Carbohydrates: 2.4 g, Dietary Fiber: 1.2 g, Total Sugars: 0.5 g

INGREDIENTS

1 Tbsp. avocado oil (optional; use if your mixture doesn't want to bind)

1 cup chopped celery

1 Tbsp. chia seeds

½ tsp. chili powder (or 1 tsp. finely minced jalapeno)

¼ cup coconut flour (or a mixture of almond and coconut flour)

1 tsp. cumin powder

1 Tbsp. dried onion flakes

½ cup finely minced cilantro leaves

4 finely minced garlic cloves

2 cups riced cauliflower

salt (to taste)

2½ Tbsp. water

INSTRUCTIONS

1. Preheat oven to 350°F (180°C).

2. If you cannot find pre-riced cauliflower, clean the head of cauliflower and break it into florets. Pulse florets in a food processor until the texture resembles rice. It doesn't take long to go from rice to mush, so pulse briefly and check often.

3. In a large bowl, add the cauliflower, celery, cilantro, coconut flour, garlic, jalapeno, and dried onion. Thoroughly mix all ingredients. Salt and pepper to taste and mix again.

4. The mixture should be dough-like consistency. If not, mix chia seeds and water and set aside until an egg-like mixture forms. After that happens, blend it into the cauliflower mixture and blend well. Add salt if desired.

5. With a greased palm, pull out a small amount of dough and roll it into a ball. Squish it slightly to create small falafels.

6. Place the falafel balls on a greased baking sheet.

7. Bake the falafels for 15 to 20 minutes. The edges will be brown when they are done.

8. Preheat the air fryer to 355°F.

9. Let the falafels sit on the baking sheet for five minutes, then transfer them to a cooling rack.

10. Line the air fryer rack with parchment paper. Place falafels in the air fryer for 12-16 minutes. The balls will take on a brownish color when done.

Cauliflower & Broccoli with Tahini Sauce

This Buddha bowl is filling and tasty, with great texture and zing.

Yield: 4 servings

Calories: 277, Total Carbohydrates: 20.8 g, Dietary Fiber: 7.4 g, Total Sugars: 4.6 g

TAHINI SAUCE INGREDIENTS

½ tsp. garlic powder

3 Tbsp. lemon juice

½ tsp. salt

5 Tbsp. tahini

4-6 Tbsp. water

BOWL INGREDIENTS

2 avocados

1 tsp. avocado oil (you can also use olive or coconut oil)

black pepper (to taste)

4 cup broccoli

1 average-sized head of cauliflower

½ cup hemp seeds

3 Tbsp. lemon juice

¾ cup raw pumpkin seeds

salt (to taste)

4 cup spinach

BOWL INSTRUCTIONS

1. Preheat oven to 400°F.

2. Break the head of cauliflower into small florets and place them in a large bowl.

3. Toss the cauliflower with lemon juice, oil, and salt until the florets are thoroughly and evenly coated. Spread the coated florets onto a baking sheet and roast for 30 minutes.

4. At the same time, boil a small amount of water in a large pan and insert a metal strainer in the pan. Put the broccoli in the strainer and cover it with the pan's lid. Allow it to boil for about eight minutes. When broccoli is ready, you can pierce the stalks easily with a fork, and your kitchen will smell like it has gastrointestinal issues.

5. While the cauliflower and broccoli are cooking, prepare the tahini sauce according to the instructions below.

6. Ready four bowls and line them each with a cup of spinach.

7. Place one half of an avocado in each bowl and evenly distribute the hemp and pumpkin seeds between them.

8. Top with the desired amount of tahini dressing and serve immediately. Extra bowls will stay fresh for up to two days if stored in an airtight container in the refrigerator.

TAHINI SAUCE INSTRUCTIONS

9. Whisk the garlic powder, lemon juice, salt, tahini, and four tablespoons of water until the mixture is smooth and creamy. Add additional water if needed to make the consistency pourable.

Baked Cauliflower Florets

These can be served with vegan gorgonzola, Roquefort, or warm, dairy-free yogurt.

Yield: 3 servings

INGREDIENTS

1 cup almond flour

1 bunch of chopped parsley

1 cup buffalo sauce

1 Tbsp. coconut oil

1 tsp. garlic powder

2 Tbsp. grated scallion whites

1 head of cauliflower

¼ tsp. sea salt

½ cup unsweetened almond milk

INSTRUCTIONS

1. Preheat oven to 375°F.

2. Line a baking sheet with parchment paper.

3. In a large bowl, mix the almond flour, garlic powder, shallot, and salt. Add almond milk gradually while constantly stirring.

4. When the blend has the consistency of a batter, mix in cauliflower florets, and coat them thoroughly.

5. Line the coated florets in a single layer on the baking tray and bake for 30 minutes. Florets will be golden brown when done.

6. While the florets are cooking, mix the Buffalo sauce and coconut oil in a medium-sized bowl. Set it aside.

7. After removing the baking tray from the oven, drizzle the Buffalo sauce mix over the florets and roll them around with a fork to coat them evenly.

8. Bake for 15 more minutes.

9. After removing the baking tray again, sprinkle chopped parsley over the florets and serve.

NUTRITIONAL INFORMATION (PER SERVING)

Calories: 331, Total Carbohydrates: 23.8 g, Dietary Fiber: 8.2 g, Total Sugars: 7 g

Mexican Chili Stew

They're diced into relatively similar chunks to ensure the vegetables cook evenly. Chili can be served with parsley garnish and/or lime wedges. Avocado slices will minimally increase the calories and carbohydrates but add texture and flavor.

Yield: 2 servings

INGREDIENTS

2 diced bell peppers

2 diced stalks of celery

1 diced turnip

2 tsp. ground cumin

2 crushed garlic cloves

1 cup cooked chickpeas/lupini beans

1 Tbsp. olive oil

¼ cup roughly chopped scallion whites

1 tsp. red chili flakes

¼ tsp. sea salt

14.5 oz. (400 g) can of diced tomatoes (with juices)

2 Tbsp. tomato sauce

1 cup walnuts

¼ cup (60 ml) water

INSTRUCTIONS

1. In a medium-sized frying pan, heat the olive oil over medium heat.

2. Add the bell peppers, celery, chickpeas, garlic, scallions, turnip, and walnuts to the frying pan and stir for five minutes.

3. Mix in the cumin and red chili flakes, stirring for one more minute.

4. Pour in the entire can of diced tomatoes, tomato sauce, and water. Keep stirring until it has come to a boil, then reduce heat to low and allow to simmer for 10 minutes.

NUTRITIONAL INFORMATION (PER SERVING)

Calories: 598, Total Carbohydrates: 33.2 g, Dietary Fiber: 10.7 g, Total Sugars: 16.3 g

Stir-Fried Mushrooms with Vegetables

A flavorful and nutritious alternative to traditional stir-fry, this recipe takes a little prep but isn't difficult to make.

Yield: 4 servings

INGREDIENTS

¼ cup cashews

½ cup chopped celery

1 Tbsp. coconut sugar

¼ tsp. crushed red pepper flakes

1 Tbsp. dried onion flakes

2 tsp. freshly grated ginger

2 Tbsp. low-sodium soy sauce

3 minced garlic cloves

2 Tbsp. rice wine vinegar

1 Tbsp. sesame seeds

½ cup shredded turnips

2 cups sliced mushrooms

2 cups small broccoli florets

¼ cup (60 ml) vegetable broth

INSTRUCTIONS

1. Combine the broccoli, celery, garlic, ginger, mushrooms, onion flakes, red pepper flakes, and water in a large frying pan over high heat.

2. Stir frequently and cook until vegetables are tender. Add vegetable broth gradually to keep vegetables from sticking to the pan.

3. Add cashews, coconut sugar, soy sauce, turnips, and vinegar. Mix well and simmer for two minutes. Sprinkle sesame seeds over the pan and serve.

NUTRITIONAL INFORMATION (PER SERVING)

Calories: 124, Total Carbohydrates: 14.9 g, Dietary Fiber: 2.8 g, Total Sugars: 6.7 g

Zoodles with Creamy Mushrooms

Using zucchini noodles (zoodles) instead of traditional pasta makes this old favorite brand new again (and much healthier).

Yield: 4 servings

NUTRITIONAL INFORMATION (PER SERVING)

Calories: 207, Total Carbohydrates: 17 g, Dietary Fiber: 5 g, Total Sugars: 6.6 g

INGREDIENTS

2 bay leaves

black pepper (to taste)

3 Tbsp. almond flour

½ tsp. Dijon mustard

½ cup dry white wine

3 Tbsp. finely diced scallion whites

6 finely minced garlic cloves

fresh, finely chopped parsley (for garnish)

2 tsp. fresh thyme

2 Tbsp. nutritional yeast

salt (to taste)

2 tsp. Soy sauce

10 oz. (300 g) thickly sliced mushrooms

4 cups (960 ml) vegan beef broth

½ cup (120 ml) vegan sour cream

2 zucchinis

INSTRUCTIONS

1. Spiralize the zucchini and cut the zoodles into the desired length. Gently press the zoodles dry with a paper towel. Bring a large pot of salty water to a boil and add the zoodles for one to two minutes. Pull the zoodles out with tongs and immediately drop them into a large bowl of ice water. After about 30 seconds, drain the zoodles and set them aside.

2. Heat a medium pot over medium heat and add two tablespoons of broth. Add garlic and onion flakes as soon as the broth is warm. Sauté for about three minutes. Add more broth, a couple of tablespoons at a time, as necessary, to prevent garlic from burning.

3. Add the mushrooms and cook them for about three minutes, until they soften and begin to brown.

4. Mix in the almond flour and stir continuously for two minutes.

5. Pour in the wine and mix thoroughly. Cook for one more minute.

6. Mix well with the bay leaves, mustard, soy sauce, thyme, and yeast.

7. Slowly add broth, continuously stirring, until the mixture is smooth.

8. Over medium-low heat, simmer the mixture for about five minutes.

9. Add zoodles and simmer for five more minutes or until the zoodles have an al dente texture. Stir often to ensure the zoodles don't stick to the bottom of the pot.

10. Extract the pot from the heat and evenly mix in the sour cream.

11. Season with pepper and salt, and garnish with chopped parsley.

Grilled Eggplant

Vegetables don't have to be boring! This recipe brings amazing flavor to a very keto-friendly veggie.

Yield: 4 servings

INGREDIENTS

1 tsp. Aleppo pepper

2 Tbsp. chopped, fresh mint

2 Tbsp. chopped parsley

1 globe eggplant

1 tsp. finely minced garlic

2 tsp. lemon juice

4 Tbsp. olive oil

2 tsp. red wine vinegar

2 tsp. sea salt

INSTRUCTIONS

1. Wash the eggplant and discard the stem end, but do not peel. Cut it evenly into slices about three-quarter inches thick.

2. Double up a layer of paper towels and layout the eggplant slices in a single layer. Sprinkle one teaspoon of salt over the slices.

3. Let the slices drain excess moisture for 20 minutes.

4. On a new double layer of paper towels, flip the slices and repeat, sprinkling one teaspoon of salt and letting them drain for 20 more minutes.

5. While the eggplant slices drain, mix the garlic, lemon juice, olive oil, Aleppo pepper, and red wine vinegar with a whisk, creating the spicy sauce.

6. Preheat a grill (gas or charcoal) to medium-high heat.

7. After both sides of the eggplant slices have drained, layer fresh paper towels over the top and press down with your hands to remove more moisture.

8. Wipe each slice of eggplant dry and brush each side with olive oil. Lay them out on a baking sheet.

9. Transfer the slices to the grill and cook on each side for four to five minutes. Watch closely to make sure they don't overcook.

10. After cooking, replace the slices on the baking sheet in a single layer and ladle sauce over each slice. Let the slices absorb the sauce for 10 to 15 minutes.

11. Sprinkle slices with mint and parsley; serve warm.

NUTRITIONAL INFORMATION (PER SERVING)

Calories: 158, Total Carbohydrates: 8.7 g, Dietary Fiber: 5.1 g, Total Sugars: 4.2 g

Bigos with Mushrooms

By making small substitutions (turnips instead of carrots, scallion whites instead of red onions), you can have some of your favorite recipes and still stay on track.

Yield: 2 servings

INGREDIENTS

black pepper (to taste)

2 chopped celery stalks

chopped scallion greens (for garnish)

2 Tbsp. chopped scallion whites

1 Tbsp. olive oil

¼ tsp. sea salt

sesame seeds (for garnish)

4 cups shredded cabbage

1 cup shredded turnip

1 cup sliced mushrooms

2 Tbsp. soy sauce

1 tsp. toasted sesame seed oil

tofu (optional)

water

INSTRUCTIONS

1. Heat the olive oil over medium-high heat in a Dutch oven or large, deep frying pan.

2. Sauté the celery, scallions, and turnips for about five minutes or until they soften.

3. Add the cabbage, mushrooms, pepper, salt, soy sauce, and a dash of water to keep the vegetables from sticking to the pan. This should immediately produce steam.

4. Cover the pan and turn the heat to medium-low. Cook for 10 - 15 minutes until the vegetables reach your desired tenderness.

5. Add the sesame oil.

6. If you want to add tofu, scoot the vegetable mix to the sides of the pan, creating a pit in the center. Add a small additional amount of olive oil and pressed tofu. Scramble the tofu with a spatula, then mix it with the vegetables.

7. Sprinkle mixture with salt and pepper to taste, then top with the green onions and sesame seeds.

NUTRITIONAL INFORMATION (PER SERVING)

Calories: 202, Total Carbohydrates: 21 g, Dietary Fiber: 4.7 g, Total Sugars: 6.9 g

Vegan Mushroom Shepherd's Pie

I know, I know…vegan *and* keto-friendly shepherd's pie? Believe it or not, this favorite comfort food can be yours.

Yield: 4 servings

NUTRITIONAL INFORMATION (PER SERVING)

Calories: 262, Total Carbohydrates: 25.5 g, Dietary Fiber: 9.2 g, Total Sugars: 9.9 g

1½ lb. cauliflower

3 chopped garlic cloves

2 diced celery stalks

1 cup diced turnips

1 Tbsp. Dijon mustard

3 Tbsp. dried onion flakes

1 lb. diced fresh mushrooms

½ cup dried wild mushrooms

1 pinch of ground nutmeg

3 Tbsp. nutritional yeast

4 Tbsp. olive oil

pepper (to taste)

5 tsp. roughly chopped thyme leaves

1 tsp. sea salt (plus more to taste)

1 Tbsp. tomato paste

1 cup (240 ml) vegetable stock

water

¼ cup red wine

1. Preheat oven to 400°F.

2. Measure two and a half tablespoons of boiling water and pour it into a bowl. Add the wild mushrooms and set them aside.

3. Chop the cauliflower into florets, keeping them as equally sized as possible.

4. Add the cauliflower to a large saucepan and cover it with water before turning on high heat. Sprinkle in a pinch of salt and bring to a boil. Cook for about five minutes or until the cauliflower is tender, then drain.

5. Heat a large frying pan over medium heat and add the celery, olive oil, onion flakes, and turnips. Stir often, cooking until the vegetables are golden.

6. Separate the fresh mushrooms into six parts. Add one part at a time to the frying pan, ensuring each part is cooked before the next part is added.

7. Drain the wild mushrooms and set the mushroom water aside. Roughly chop the wild mushrooms and add them to the frying pan with tomato paste. Increase heat to medium-high.

8. Stir the vegetables and add the red wine, cooking until the wine has almost evaporated. Add the wild mushroom water and vegetable stock.

9. Reduce heat to low. Simmer until approximately half of the liquid has been absorbed, then remove from heat.

10. Put the cauliflower, mustard, nutritional yeast, olive oil, salt, and thyme into a food processor or blender and pureé until smooth. Taste the cauliflower mix and adjust the seasoning as desired. Add the nutmeg and blend for an additional minute.

11. Separate the mushroom mix between four ramekins and cover with the cauliflower blend. Bake for 20 minutes. The tops should be golden when finished.

Fried Shirataki Noodles with Broccolini

Like zoodles, shirataki noodles are a fantastic, adaptable option for a keto-friendly diet, and they can be paired with any of the sauce recipes in this book.

Yield: 1 serving

INGREDIENTS

- 1 Tbsp. almond butter
- 3½ oz. (100 g) broccolini
- 2 Tbsp. coconut aminos
- 3 diced scallions
- 2 minced garlic cloves
- 1 Tbsp. olive oil or coconut oil
- 8 oz. (220 g) shirataki noodles
- ¼ cup shredded cabbage
- 1 - 2 tsp. sriracha sauce
- 1 turnip cut into batons

INSTRUCTIONS

1. Warm the olive oil over medium heat in a wok or large saucepan.
2. Add the garlic and scallions and cook them until softened.
3. Add in the rest of the vegetables.
4. Rinse the noodles thoroughly with warm water and add them to the vegetables.
5. When the vegetables are starting to become tender, add almond butter, coconut aminos, and sriracha. Stir well until warm.

NUTRITIONAL INFORMATION (PER SERVING)

Calories: 372, Total Carbohydrates: 32.8 g, Dietary Fiber: 10.9 g, Total Sugars: 7.4 g

Grilled Marinated Mushrooms

Backyard barbecues are rife with keto-friendly meal options, but vegan fare. Not so much. These Portobello steaks can fill that gap.

Yield: 4 servings

INGREDIENTS

3 Tbsp. balsamic vinegar

fresh cracked pepper (to taste)

½ tsp. granulated onion

2 Tbsp. grapeseed oil

4 large Portobello mushrooms

1 - 2 tsp. liquid smoke

1 minced garlic clove

sea salt (to taste)

3 Tbsp. soy sauce

1 Tbsp. vegan Worcestershire sauce

INSTRUCTIONS

1. Remove the stems from the mushrooms, and dry brush them with a dry pastry brush or a paper towel wad. The drier the mushrooms are, the better they will sear.

2. Add all the ingredients to a large, shallow baking dish except for the mushrooms and oil. Whisk the ingredients together to create a marinade and taste. Add additional seasonings if desired.

3. Add the mushrooms to the baking dish and liberally rub the marinade over all the mushrooms' surfaces.

4. Let the mushrooms marinate in the baking dish for 10 to 20 minutes.

5. Heat a grill or frying pan to medium-high heat.

6. When the grill or pan is thoroughly heated, brush the cooking surface with oil and place the mushrooms down with plenty of space between them.

7. Delicately press the mushrooms into the grill/pan with tongs or a spatula and hold for four to five minutes to allow the mushrooms to sear.

8. Flip the mushrooms over and repeat on the other side, applying more oil if needed. More marinade can be spooned onto mushrooms for a more robust flavor.

NUTRITIONAL INFORMATION (PER SERVING)

Calories: 95, Total Carbohydrates: 5.4 g, Dietary Fiber: 1.3 g, Total Sugars: 1 g

Salad Recipes

Salad should be a no-brainer for a vegan keto meal, but it can get very boring quickly. After all, there are only so many ways you can combine leafy greens and low-carb veggies without feeling like you're eating your way through *Groundhog Day*. These are some options to keep the dietary goals without sacrificing variety.

Kale Avocado Salad

Summer Salad

Red Cabbage Salad

Mediterranean Artichoke Salad

Kale Avocado Salad

This can also be topped with pine nuts, sunflower or hemp seeds, chopped parsley, and/or chives.

Yield: 6 servings

INGREDIENTS

2 avocados

1 Tbsp. avocado oil

2 tsp. capers

¾ cup walnuts

1 cup chopped iceberg lettuce

4 cups chopped kale (ribs removed)

4 cups chopped romaine lettuce

1 tsp. Dijon mustard

1 garlic clove

2 Tbsp. lemon juice

3 Tbsp. nutritional yeast

¼ tsp. sea salt

⅓ cup (160 ml) water

INSTRUCTIONS

1. Place the kale into a bowl and massage the avocado oil by hand until it softens and darkens in color.

2. To make the dressing, pureé capers, walnuts, garlic, lemon juice, mustard, nutritional yeast, salt, and one-third cup of water in a food processor or high-speed blender. Mix until smooth and creamy. Add salt and pepper to taste.

3. Cut the avocados into large pieces.

4. Mix the avocado, kale, iceberg, and romaine with the dressing of your choice.

NUTRITIONAL INFORMATION (PER SERVING)

Calories: 211, Total Carbohydrates: 18.4 g, Dietary Fiber: 5.8 g, Total Sugars: 2.7 g

Summer Salad

This easy, tangy recipe has some great zip and is a nice change of pace from leafy salads.

Yield: 10 servings

INGREDIENTS

- ¼ tsp. black pepper (more to taste)
- 2 large cucumbers
- 4 large tomatoes
- ¼ cup almonds
- ¼ cup cashews
- ¼ cup (60 ml) olive oil
- ¼ cup (60 ml) red wine vinegar
- ½ tsp. sea salt (more to taste)

INSTRUCTIONS

1. Chop the vegetables into bite-sized pieces and toss them together in a large bowl.
2. Mix the oil, pepper, salt, and vinegar in a small bowl with a whisk to create a dressing.
3. Pour the dressing over the vegetables and toss again to coat them thoroughly.
4. Allow the salad to sit for at least 20 minutes before serving to allow the vegetables to absorb the flavor of the dressing. Sprinkle with nuts.

NUTRITIONAL INFORMATION (PER SERVING)

Calories: 67, Total Carbohydrates: 5.1 g, Dietary Fiber: 1.2 g, Total Sugars: 2.9 g

Red Cabbage Salad

This salad is, pardon the term, meatier than a lot of leafy green salads, so it's very filling.

Yield: 6 servings

SALAD INGREDIENTS

2 Tbsp. chopped pecans

¼ cup finely diced scallion whites

3 Tbsp. grated turnips

3 Tbsp. roasted sunflower seeds

¼ cup shredded red cabbage

2 Tbsp. sliced almonds

5 cups small broccoli florets

DRESSING INGREDIENTS

3 Tbsp. apple cider vinegar

½ tsp. garlic powder

1 pinch of black pepper

2 Tbsp. plain, dairy-free yogurt

½ tsp. sea salt

3 Tbsp. sunflower seed butter

water (if necessary to thin dressing)

SALAD INSTRUCTIONS

1. Add the broccoli florets, cabbage, and scallion whites, and turnips into a large mixing bowl with half the seeds and nuts. Set it aside.

2. Make the dressing according to the instructions below.

3. Pour half of the dressing over the salad and toss well, coating evenly.

4. Refrigerate and chill for 40 minutes or more.

5. Immediately before serving, add the remaining dressing, nuts, and seeds, and toss thoroughly.

DRESSING INSTRUCTIONS

6. Add all the dressing ingredients to another large mixing bowl and whisk briskly or mix with a hand mixer.

7. Taste and adjust spices if desired. If the dressing is too thick, add small amounts of water until it is the appropriate viscosity.

NUTRITIONAL INFORMATION (PER SERVING)

Calories: 133, Total Carbohydrates: 10 g, Dietary Fiber: 3.1 g, Total Sugars: 2.1 g

Mediterranean Artichoke Salad

In the mood for Italian food but need to skip the pasta, meat, and cheese? This salad will scratch that itch.

Yield: 6 servings

INGREDIENTS

- ¼ tsp. crushed red pepper
- ½ tsp. dried oregano
- ½ tsp. dried parsley
- 2 Tbsp. extra virgin olive oil
- ¼ tsp. garlic powder
- 1 cup halved grape tomatoes
- 1½ cups marinated artichoke hearts cut into bite-size pieces
- 2 figs, sliced
- ¼ cup scallion whites cut into thin coins
- 1 cucumber, sliced
- ½ tsp. sea salt
- ½ Tbsp. white wine vinegar

INSTRUCTIONS

1. Combine all the vegetables in a large bowl.
2. In a smaller bowl, combine the garlic powder, oil, oregano, parsley, pepper, salt, and vinegar and briskly whisk until the dressing emulsifies.
3. Coat vegetables with the dressing and serve.

NUTRITIONAL INFORMATION (PER SERVING)

Calories: 83, Total Carbohydrates: 4.9 g, Dietary Fiber: 1.5 g, Total Sugars: 1.4 g

Soup Recipes

Nothing beats a warm bowl of soup on a cold day, but so many are filled with high-carb veggies like carrots or loads of lentils or have a milk-based cream as a staple ingredient that it can be difficult to find appetizing options. Luckily for you, this chapter has five!

Pisto Manchego

Five Ingredient Miso Soup

Cream of Broccoli Soup

Tender Cauliflower Soup with Cashews

Cream Tomato Soup

Pisto Manchego

This delicious stew can also have cauliflower or turnips added to the recipe for further nutrients.

Yield: 3 servings

INGREDIENTS

1 Tbsp. balsamic vinegar

1 bell pepper

black pepper (to taste)

1 tsp. brown sugar replacement

1 large eggplant

3 minced garlic cloves

¼ tsp. ground ginger

1 Tbsp. olive oil

3 Tbsp. finely chopped scallions

½ tsp. dried oregano

1⅓ tsp. smoked paprika

¼ tsp. red pepper flakes

¼ cup (60 ml) red wine

¾ tsp. sea salt (more to taste)

roughly chopped fresh thyme (to taste)

3 tomatoes

1 Tbsp. tomato paste

1 large zucchini

INSTRUCTIONS

1. Cut the bell pepper, eggplant, tomatoes, and zucchini into one-inch pieces.

2. Heat the oil in a large frying pan over medium heat and sauté the scallions until golden brown, roughly four to five minutes.

3. Add eggplant and garlic to the pan and cook for three to four minutes.

4. Reduce heat to medium-low.

5. Add the brown sugar replacement, ginger, red pepper, oregano, paprika, salt, and wine to the pan and let it simmer for five to six minutes, occasionally stirring.

6. Add the bell peppers, tomatoes, and zucchini to the pan and cook until the vegetables are tender.

7. If more broth is desired, add additional wine.

8. Add the tomato paste and vinegar. Stir to combine. If a thicker broth is desired, add more paste.

9. Sample and adjust seasonings to taste. Sprinkle thyme over the stew and serve.

NUTRITIONAL INFORMATION (PER SERVING)

Calories: 146, Total Carbohydrates: 26.8 g, Dietary Fiber: 9.7 g, Total Sugars: 14.5 g

Five Ingredient Miso Soup

This one is a favorite, if only because it is so intensely simple! No joke, five ingredients, and none of them are obscure or hard to find! Make cooking this even easier on yourself by buying pre-minced garlic. Having it on hand saves a lot of time and effort, regardless of how easy the recipe is.

Yield: 2 servings

INGREDIENTS

½ cup chopped kale

½ cup chopped scallions

3 Tbsp. light yellow miso

2 minced garlic cloves

water

INSTRUCTIONS

1. In a small mixing bowl, gradually mix very small amounts of warm water to the miso with a whisk until it has the consistency of a smooth paste.
2. In a saucepan over high heat, bring four cups of water to a low simmer.
3. Reduce heat to maintain the simmer and add the miso paste. Stir well.
4. Add the garlic, kale, and scallions to the saucepan.
5. Simmer for five minutes.

NUTRITIONAL INFORMATION (PER SERVING)

Calories: 72, Total Carbohydrates: 11.4 g, Dietary Fiber: 2.4 g, Total Sugars: 2.2 g

Cream of Broccoli Soup

Don't be fooled by the 'cream' in this cream of broccoli. Although it is creamy, it's also completely vegan. You can always substitute the turnips for cauliflower—they produce a similar texture when cooked.

Yield: 6 servings

NUTRITIONAL INFORMATION (PER SERVING)

Calories: 134, Total Carbohydrates: 19.3 g, Dietary Fiber: 5.3 g, Total Sugars: 6.2 g

INGREDIENTS

1 diced leek

¼ cup diced shallot whites

3 tsp. garlic powder

2 large heads of broccoli

3 minced garlic cloves

¼ cup nutritional yeast

3 tsp. onion powder

3 Tbsp. soy sauce

4 thickly chopped celery stalks

3 thickly chopped turnips

6 cups (1440 ml) vegetable broth

INSTRUCTIONS

1. Bring a large pot of water to a boil. Add the celery and turnips, and boil uncovered for 30 minutes. The vegetables should be soft enough to pierce easily with a fork.

2. Drain the vegetables and place them in a food processor or high-speed blender with two cups of broth, garlic powder, onion powder, soy sauce, and yeast, then pour one more cup of broth over the rest of the ingredients.

3. Pureé until completely smooth; this is your cheese base.

4. Keep half the cheese base in the food processor/blender and place half into the pan used to cook the celery and turnips.

5. Remove stems from the broccoli and cut the crowns into large florets.

6. Steam the broccoli florets for eight minutes or until very tender.

7. Place half of the steamed broccoli into the food processor/blender with the cheese base and pureé until creamy and smooth.

8. Pour that mixture into the other half of the cheese base.

9. Chop the remaining steamed broccoli into rough, uneven pieces, and set aside.

10. Sauté the leeks and shallots in a large frying pan with a small amount of broth to prevent them from sticking to the pan.

11. Cook the vegetables until tender and translucent, then add them to the cheese base.

12. Add the chopped broccoli and remaining broth to the cheese base and turn on low heat, stirring until the soup is heated.

Tender Cauliflower Soup with Cashews

This is another super sneaky soup. All the rich texture of cream with none of the actual cream.

Yield: 6 servings

INGREDIENTS

1 cup chopped celery

3 cups chopped kale, ribs removed (spinach can be used as a substitute)

3 Tbsp. chopped scallion whites

4 diced turnips

1 lb. (450 g) fresh or frozen cauliflower florets

4 minced garlic cloves

¾ cup raw cashews

6 cups (1440 ml) vegetable broth

INSTRUCTIONS

1. Soak the cashews in boiling water for five minutes. Set them aside.

2. Using a large pot, sauté the scallions in a few tablespoons of broth until tender and translucent, about three to five minutes.

3. Add the celery, garlic, and turnips. Sauté for several more minutes, then add the vegetable broth and cauliflower. Bring this soup mix to a boil and cook for 10 to 15 minutes. Remove from heat.

4. Place the soaked cashews and one cup of the soup mix into a food processor or high-speed blender. Pureé until smooth and then return to the rest of the soup.

5. By degrees, purée all the soup in the food processor or blender until it has a creamy texture. If you have an immersion blender, you can do this all at once in the pot.

6. Add the kale to the pot and stir well. Let the soup simmer for roughly 10 minutes. If you have substituted spinach, only simmer until the leaves wilt.

7. If you prefer less texture to the soup, blend it again after the added greens.

NUTRITIONAL INFORMATION (PER SERVING)

Calories: 202, Total Carbohydrates: 20.7 g, Dietary Fiber: 4.6 g, Total Sugars: 7 g

Cream Tomato Soup

This soup has a velvety texture and rich flavor. It pairs well with the tortilla chips in Chapter six.

Yield: 4 servings

INGREDIENTS

27 oz. (760 ml) canned, whole peeled tomatoes

3 Tbsp. dried onion flakes

1 cup finely chopped celery

2 finely chopped garlic cloves

¼ cup tightly packed fresh basil leaves

1 tsp. maple syrup

2 Tbsp. olive oil

½ cup raw cashews

¾ tsp. sea salt

2 Tbsp. tomato paste

2 cups (480 ml) vegetable broth

INSTRUCTIONS

1. Add celery, garlic, oil, onion flakes, and salt in a large pot over medium heat. Sauté for roughly seven minutes until the celery is softened. Stir in tomato paste and combine.

2. Add the canned tomatoes and bring to a mellow simmer. Allow to simmer uncovered for 10 minutes.

3. Pour the soup into a food processor or high-speed blender, gradually adding the cashews and syrup. Begin blending slowly, then increase to higher speeds for about two minutes until the soup is creamy and smooth.

4. Add the basil to the food processor/blender. Depending on how much texture you would like, either pulse the leaves several times or pureé until smooth.

NUTRITIONAL INFORMATION (PER SERVING)

Calories: 244, Total Carbohydrates: 20.4 g, Dietary Fiber: 3.2 g, Total Sugars: 9.3 g

Sauces and Dressings

A good sauce or dressing can transform a meal. Here are some ideas for dressing your veggies and perking up your taste buds.

Cream Sauce

Fresh Pesto

Lemon Ranch Dressing

Cream Sauce

This extremely easy recipe adds a lot of flavors to anything from steamed broccoli to jicama fries.

Yield: 6¼ cups servings

INGREDIENTS

¾ cup (180 ml) almond milk

1 Tbsp. coconut flour

2 Tbsp. Dijon mustard

½ tsp. garlic powder

2 Tbsp. low-sodium soy sauce

6 Tbsp. nutritional yeast

½ tsp. onion powder

sea salt (to taste)

INSTRUCTIONS

1. In a large mixing bowl, briskly whisk all the ingredients together. Done.

2. I'm serious, you're finished.

NUTRITIONAL INFORMATION (PER SERVING)

Calories: 121, Total Carbohydrates: 8.5 g, Dietary Fiber: 4.2 g, Total Sugars: 1.7 g

Fresh Pesto

This is a great topper on zoodles or shirataki noodles. You can also drizzle it over fresh tomatoes for extra flavor.

Yield: 6 servings

INGREDIENTS

fresh ground pepper (to taste)

1 garlic clove

kosher salt (to taste)

1 Tbsp. lemon juice

3 cups lightly packed basil leaves, stems removed

¼ cup lightly toasted pine nuts

½ tsp. nutritional yeast

¼ – ½ cup olive oil

INSTRUCTIONS

1. In a food processor or high-speed blender, grind the basil, lemon juice, nutritional yeast, pepper, and pine nuts on a pulse for 30 seconds to break up the ingredients.

2. Pour in a fourth of a cup of the oil and turn the food processor/blender on high for 30 more seconds. Sample and adjust pepper and salt to taste.

3. Add additional oil if a thinner texture is desired, and blend to mix.

NUTRITIONAL INFORMATION (PER SERVING)

Calories: 115, Total Carbohydrates: 1.4 g, Dietary Fiber: 0.5 g, Total Sugars: 0.3 g

Lemon Ranch Dressing

Who doesn't love a creamy ranch? Go forth and drown all the celery and cucumbers you can get your hands on in this delicious version.

Yield: 20 servings

INGREDIENTS

½ tsp. dried dill

1 tsp. dried parsley

2 Tbsp. finely chopped fresh chives

1 tsp. garlic powder

3 Tbsp. lemon juice

1 tsp. onion powder

1½ cups raw cashews, soaked for an hour

½ – 1 tsp. sea salt

1 cup (240 ml) water

INSTRUCTIONS

1. In a food processor or high-speed blender, pureé the soaked cashews, garlic powder, lemon juice, onion powder, salt, and water on high until the mixture is creamy.

2. Pour the mixture into a storage container and gently stir in chives, dill, and parsley.

3. After refrigeration, the dressing will thicken and must be stirred before serving.

NUTRITIONAL INFORMATION (PER SERVING)

Calories: 54, Total Carbohydrates: 3.3 g, Dietary Fiber: 0.3 g, Total Sugars: 0.6 g

Snacks

Let's face it, if you're going to fall off the keto boat, snack time is the most likely time for that to happen. Having guilt-free snacks at hand can save you from less carb-friendly options.

Organic Jicama Fries

Nachos Chips

Oven-Baked Zucchini Chips

Savory Spiced Pecans

Organic Jicama Fries

These are great when you're craving traditional potato fries. All the satisfying flavor, no starchy regret. You can experiment with some different spices for many flavorful variations.

Yield: 6 servings

INGREDIENTS

5 tsp. avocado oil

2 tsp. fresh, finely chopped parsley

¼ tsp. garlic powder

½ tsp. ground turmeric

⅛ tsp. onion powder

¼ tsp. paprika

15 oz. (420 g) raw jicama

1½ tsp. sea salt

2½ (600 ml) cup water

INSTRUCTIONS

1. Preheat oven to 400°F.

2. Line a baking sheet with foil.

3. Peel off the skin from the jicama with a vegetable peeler and cut the jicama into a standard fry shape.

4. Bring the water and half a teaspoon of salt to a boil in a medium saucepan over high heat. Add the jicama fries.

5. Cover the pan and boil for 10 minutes.

6. Drain the jicama and place it in a large mixing bowl. Coat the fries with the avocado oil and toss with the garlic powder, paprika, onion powder, remaining salt, and turmeric. Ensure the fries are completely glazed with spices and add more if you want a more robust flavor.

7. Arrange the fries on a baking pan in a single layer and bake for 20 minutes.

8. Remove the pan, flip each fry over, and place it in the oven to bake for 20 more minutes.

9. Allow the fries to cool a little before garnishing them with parsley.

NUTRITIONAL INFORMATION (PER SERVING)

Calories: 35, Total Carbohydrates: 7.1 g, Dietary Fiber: 3.8 g, Total Sugars: 1.5 g

Nachos Chips

Bust out your old-school Play-Doh skills to make some crunchy munchies! These are savory snacks that will satisfy you when you need a crunch, and they can be modified with any spices that suit your mood.

Yield: 30 chips

NUTRITIONAL INFORMATION (PER SERVING)

Calories: 28, Total Carbohydrates: 1.1 g, Dietary Fiber: 0.6 g, Total Sugars: 0.1 g

INGREDIENTS

1 cup almond flour	¼ tsp. ground cumin
1 Tbsp. chia seeds	1 tsp. nutritional yeast
1 Tbsp. extra virgin olive oil	¼ tsp. sea salt
¼ tsp. garlic powder	¼ cup (60 ml) water

INSTRUCTIONS

1. Preheat oven to 390°F.

2. Set aside two large sheets of parchment paper.

3. Mix the chia seeds and water in a small bowl with a whisk. Set aside until it develops into a gel-like texture, roughly 10 minutes.

4. When the chia mixture has set, combine it with the almond flour, olive oil, and spices in a larger mixing bowl.

5. Knead all of it together with your hands. Enthusiastically squeeze the mixture with your fingers to blend chia gel and almond flour, creating a dough. In about one minute, you should have a dough ball.

6. Place the ball between the sheets of parchment paper and roll as thinly as you can with a rolling pin.

7. Remove the top sheet of parchment paper.

8. With a sharp knife or pizza cutter, slice dough into strips. You can also use cookie cutters for more original shapes. If you want traditional wedge-shaped chips, place a plate on the dough and cut off the excess dough around it to make a dough circle. Cut the circle into pie slices. Roll the extra dough back out and repeat until all the dough is used, but it is important to keep the same consistency in thickness so that the chips will cook evenly.

9. With the parchment paper, move the raw chips to a baking sheet and place them in the oven.

10. Bake for five minutes and check the chip color. They should be golden brown. Very thin chips can take up to seven minutes to cook fully, while thicker chips can take up to nine minutes. If you need more than five minutes, check every 60 seconds to avoid burning.

Oven-Baked Zucchini Chips

The great thing about this simple recipe is that a huge variety of flavors can be achieved by adding different combinations of whatever spices sound tasty at any given time.

Yield: 4 servings

INGREDIENTS

1½ tsp. olive oil

½ tsp. sea salt

3 zucchinis

INSTRUCTIONS

1. Preheat oven to 200°F.

2. Using a very sharp knife or mandolin slicer, cut the zucchini into thin, even slices, discarding the ends.

3. In a large mixing bowl, coat the slices with oil, salt (and any other desired seasonings).

4. Arrange the slices in a single layer on a baking sheet and bake for one hour and 15 minutes.

5. Turn the baking sheet and bake for an additional hour and 15 minutes.

6. After two and a half hours of baking, turn off the heat, but leave the chips in the oven as it cools as they will continue to crisp.

7. Store the chips in the refrigerator in an airtight container.

NUTRITIONAL INFORMATION (PER SERVING)

Calories: 30, Total Carbohydrates: 3.1 g, Dietary Fiber: 1 g, Total Sugars: 1.6 g

Savory Spiced Pecans

The cayenne pepper can be omitted if less heat is desired in this little treat.

Yield: 8 servings

INGREDIENTS

¼ tsp. cayenne pepper

¼ cup (60 g) extra virgin olive oil

2 tsp. fresh lemon zest

¼ tsp. garlic powder

¼ tsp. onion powder

4 cup pecans

2 tsp. pink Himalayan salt

4 Tbsp. roughly chopped fresh rosemary

¼ tsp. smoked paprika

INSTRUCTIONS

1. Preheat oven to 350°F (180°C) and line a baking sheet with foil.

2. Place the pecans in a large bowl and add the rest of the ingredients except for the lemon zest.

3. Stir the mixture and make sure that the pecans are thoroughly coated.

4. Spread the coated pecans evenly along the baking sheet and bake for five minutes.

5. Remove and stir the pecans.

6. Evenly redistribute and bake for five more minutes.

7. Repeat until the pecans are golden.

8. Remove the baking sheet from the oven and allow the pecans to cool a little, then scatter lemon zest and mix through.

9. Allow the pecans to cool completely and store them in an airtight container.

NUTRITIONAL INFORMATION (PER SERVING)

Calories: 406, Total Carbohydrates: 8.4 g, Dietary Fiber: 6.1 g, Total Sugars: 1.9 g

Desserts

The biggest setback of a keto diet is the lack of desserts! Well, have no fear because your sweet tooth *can* be satisfied without throwing your entire diet out the window.

Pumpkin Spicy Blondies

Mint Chocolate Bars

Chocolate Fudge

Delicate Chocolate Mousse

Pumpkin Cupcakes

Pumpkin Spicy Blondies

Gooey, chocolatey, pumpkin-y goodness. Pair it with a cold glass of almond milk for a guilt-free treat.

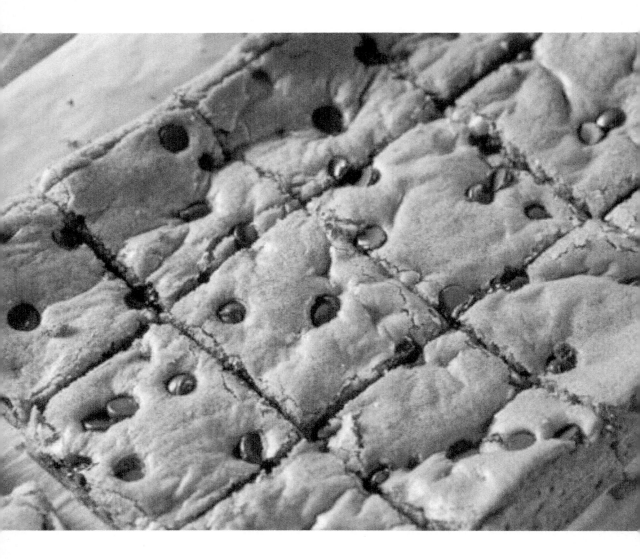

Yield: 12 bars

INGREDIENTS

½ tsp. almond extract

1 cup almond flour

1 tsp. baking soda

⅔ cup (160 g) cashew butter

¼ cup coconut flour

1 Tbsp. flaxseed

1 Tbsp. pumpkin pie spice
(plus additional for topping)

⅔ cup (160 g) pumpkin pureé

¼ tsp. sea salt

⅔ cup stevia

1 cup sugar-free chocolate chips (plus additional for topping)

3 Tbsp. water

INSTRUCTIONS

1. Preheat oven to 350°F (180°C).

2. Mix the flaxseed and water in a small bowl and let it sit for roughly five minutes until it attains a gel-like texture.

3. Line an 8"x8"-inch pan with parchment paper.

4. Combine the almond flour, baking soda, coconut flour, pumpkin pie spice, and salt in a large mixing bowl. Mix well.

5. In a second large bowl, combine the almond extract, cashew butter, flaxseed gel, pumpkin pureé, and stevia. Mix until all ingredients are fully combined and have a glossy texture.

6. Add the dry ingredients from the first bowl into the second and mix until all ingredients are fully combined into a cohesive batter.

7. Gently fold in chocolate chips with a spatula.

8. Pour the batter into the pan and smooth it into an evenly dispersed layer.

9. Sprinkle some additional chocolate chips and pumpkin pie spice over the top.

10. Bake for 30 to 35 minutes. Test by poking the center of the brownies with a toothpick. It will emerge clean when the brownies are done.

NUTRITIONAL INFORMATION (PER SERVING)

Calories: 241, Total Carbohydrates: 26.9 g, Dietary Fiber: 3.3 g, Total Sugars: 0.9 g

Chocolate Fudge

Honestly, there are only three ingredients between you and *fudge*. Hershey offers a wonderful sugar-free chocolate chip that is both vegan and keto-friendly.

Yield: 10 pieces

INGREDIENTS

- ½ cup cashew butter
- ½ cup (120 ml) coconut oil
- ½ cup sugar-free chocolate chips

INSTRUCTIONS

1. Line a 9x5 loaf pan with parchment paper.
2. Place a double boiler on medium heat.
3. Add all the ingredients to the boiler and stir until liquefied.
4. Pour the liquid fudge into the 9x5 pan and refrigerate or freeze until hardened.
5. Cut into serving pieces with a warm knife.

NUTRITIONAL INFORMATION (PER SERVING)

Calories: 225, Total Carbohydrates: 10.7 g, Dietary Fiber: 1.1 g, Total Sugars: 0 g

Delicate Chocolate Mousse

This is a great treat when you need something both chocolatey and chilly. Pair it with the whipped topping from the pumpkin cheesecake recipe for an added indulgence.

Yield: 5¼ cups servings

INGREDIENTS

13.5 oz. (380 ml) can full-fat coconut milk

1 Tbsp. regular cocoa powder

¼ cup stevia

¼ cup unsweetened cocoa powder

Optional Additions:

½ tsp. vanilla extract

¼ tsp. instant coffee

INSTRUCTIONS

1. Chill in a large mixing bowl.

2. Chill the coconut milk (and vanilla extract if using).

3. Open the can of coconut milk and drain out the water.

4. Pour only the thick crème remaining into the chilled bowl and whip with a mixer on high until stiff peaks form.

5. Add the rest of the ingredients and whip until a smooth texture is achieved.

NUTRITIONAL INFORMATION (PER SERVING)

Calories: 310, Total Carbohydrates: 12.1 g, Dietary Fiber: 1.8 g, Total Sugars: 0.2 g

Pumpkin Cupcakes

Yield: 6 individual cheesecakes

INGREDIENTS

13.5 oz. (390 ml) can coconut milk

¼ tsp. cinnamon

2 tsp. lemon juice

¼ tsp. pink Himalayan salt

½ cup (120 ml) pumpkin pureé

2 tsp. pumpkin spice

1 cup raw cashew pieces, soaked

⅓ cup + 1 Tbsp. refined coconut oil

⅜ tsp. stevia

¾ cup toasted pecans

2 tsp. vanilla extract

CRUST INSTRUCTIONS

1. Arrange six silicone cupcake liners /Mason jars on a large plate and set them aside.

2. Place the pecans in a food processor or high-speed blender and grind them at a pulse until ground coarsely. Add one tablespoon of coconut oil, cinnamon, and an eighth of a teaspoon of salt, and continue to pulse until it transforms into sticky crumbs.

3. Scoop one heaping tablespoonful of the crumbs into each cupcake liner and press it firmly into the bottom.

4. Set the plate of liners into a freezer to set.

5. Rinse food processor/blender.

FILLING INSTRUCTION

6. Soak the cashews in boiling water for at least two hours. Drain the cashews, rinse them under warm water, and dry them well.

7. Pureé the cashews in the food processor/blender until utterly smooth. Take care to scrape down the sides to ensure all the cashews are completely ground down.

8. Add the coconut milk, lemon juice, pumpkin pureé, pumpkin spice, an eighth of a teaspoon of salt, and a fourth teaspoon of stevia. Pureé until the mixture is completely smooth again. Mix in a third of a cup of coconut oil.

9. Taste the mixture and add salt and/or cinnamon and pumpkin spice as desired.

10. Remove the plate of crust-filled liners from the freezer.

11. Using an ice cream scoop, top the crusts with filling.

12. Tightly wrap each mold in tinfoil.

13. Replace the plate and cheesecakes in the freezer and allow them to freeze solid for 3 - 4 hours.

WHIPPED TOPPING INSTRUCTION

14. Refrigerate the remaining coconut milk for at least five hours.

15. Drain the water from the chilled coconut milk and place the remaining solid cream into a bowl.

16. Add an eighth of a teaspoon of stevia and the vanilla, and whip everything with a hand mixer until light and fluffy.

Mint Chocolate Bars

No oven is necessary for these mint chocolate treats! They're tasty, healthy, and easy to make. You can also substitute the stevia with any sugar-free sweetener of your choice, such as Truvia.

Yield: 16 bars

2 avocados

½ cup (120 g) coconut oil

½ cup cocoa powder

¾ cup (180 ml) melted coconut oil

½ tsp. peppermint extract

½ tsp. sea salt

4 cups shredded, unsweetened coconut

¾ cup + ⅛ tsp. stevia

1¼ tsp. vanilla extract

MINT LAYER INSTRUCTIONS

1. Spray an 8x8 pan with vegetable spray.

2. In a food processor or high-speed blender, mix the avocados, melted coconut oil, shredded coconut, peppermint extract, a quarter of a teaspoon of salt, a half cup of stevia, and three-quarters teaspoon vanilla extract until well blended. If you want the bars to have a rougher texture, hold back half of the shredded coconut until the rest of the ingredients are blended, then mix it in and pulse once or twice to mix.

3. Spread the batter evenly into the 8x8 pan and freeze while the chocolate layer is prepared.

CHOCOLATE LAYER INSTRUCTIONS

4. Melt half a cup of coconut oil and one-quarter cup of stevia over low heat in a small saucepan.

5. Remove from heat and stir in the cocoa powder, an eighth of a teaspoon of salt, and half of a teaspoon of vanilla extract, combining well.

6. Pour the chocolate over the cooled mint layer and return to the freezer until the chocolate is solid, roughly 15 minutes.

7. Cut into bars using a warm knife.

Our Recommendations

Keto Bread Machine Cookbook: Keto-Friendly Baking Recipes for Your Bread Machine

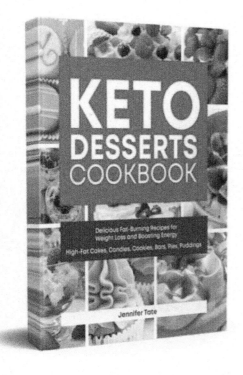

Keto Dessert Cookbook: Low-Carb Sugar-Free Recipes for Weight Loss and Boost Energy

From the Author

My name is Jennifer Tate. I have been a professional chef for over fifteen years and a passionate advocate for the ketogenic diet. I am highly recognized for making culinary magic in my home kitchen. I am also a busy mom of two. This means I am always on the run and looking for any chance to save time and money. With a passion for healthy living and first-hand knowledge of what it takes to stick to a successful lifestyle plan, I will guide you throughout this journey.

In this book, you learn exactly what the keto vegan lifestyle is and why so many people opt for this diet plan. We discussed the healing benefits and key nutritional info related to plant-based ketogenic eating.

However, consistency is key to following this diet—breakdowns can destroy the long work for your health. So, I've developed simple recipes for a keto vegan diet. I eat them myself, feed them to my family, and include them in the meal plans for my clients.

In addition to the recipes contained herein, I leave you a wide field for experiments. You can combine ingredients from the list of allowed keto products and create your masterpieces depending on your mood. But of course, don't forget the basics.

I generously share my vegan keto recipes and mastery secrets with my readers. The ketogenic plant-based diet has never been so easy-to-follow and delicious. Let yourself enjoy your food every day!

Our Recommendations

Keto Bread Cookbook: Easy Keto Bread Recipes for Low-Carb Baking to Lose Weight Fast

Keto Dessert Cookbook: Low-Carb Sugar-Free Recipes for Weight Loss and Boost Energy

Copyright

Printed in Great Britain
by Amazon

45491363R00064